Cheetahs

ABDO
Publishing Company

A Buddy Book
by
Julie Murray

VISIT US AT
www.abdopub.com

Published by Buddy Books, an imprint of ABDO Publishing Company, 4940 Viking Drive, Suite 622, Edina, Minnesota 55435. Copyright © 2005 by Abdo Consulting Group, Inc. International copyrights reserved in all countries. No part of this book may be reproduced in any form without written permission from the publisher.

Printed in the United States.

Edited by: Christy DeVillier
Contributing Editors: Matt Ray, Michael P. Goecke
Graphic Design: Maria Hosley
Image Research: Deborah Coldiron
Photographs: Corbis, Minden Pictures, Photodisc

Library of Congress Cataloging-in-Publication Data

Murray, Julie, 1969-
   Cheetahs/Julie Murray.
      p. cm. — (Animal kingdom. Set II)
   Includes bibliographical references (p.).
   Contents: Cheetahs — Cheetahs long ago — What they're like — Where they live — Size — Coat and color — Fast runners — Feeding — Cubs.
   ISBN 1-59197-305-8
      1. Cheetah—Juvenile literature. [1. Cheetah.] I. Title.

QL737.C23M877 2003
599.75'9—dc21

2003044311

Contents

Cheetahs

Cheetahs are the fastest land
animals. These large cats have been
around for thousands of years. Long
ago, people in Asia and Africa tamed
cheetahs. A king named Akbar the
Great owned about 9,000 cheetahs.

Cheetahs are the fastest cats in the world.

Coursing

Long ago, people also used cheetahs for a sport called coursing. For coursing, a blindfolded cheetah was led to an open field. The open field had gazelles and impalas. Someone removed the cheetah's blindfold. People watched the cheetah chase and catch the animals.

What They Look Like

Cheetahs are golden tan with black spots. Their tail has black stripes and a white tip. They have white fur on their belly, too. Cheetahs have black stripes on their face. These stripes are called tear marks.

Cheetahs are famous for their tear marks.

Cheetahs have a slim body and a long tail. They have long, strong legs and a large chest. Cheetahs have non-retractable claws on their feet. Non-retractable claws stay out all the time. They help cheetahs grip the ground as they run.

A cheetah's body is built for speed.

Cheetahs are smaller than lions and tigers. Male cheetahs grow to become about four feet (one m) long. Adult males stand about three feet (one m) tall. They weigh between 90 and 140 pounds (41 and 64 kg). Female cheetahs are smaller.

Where They Live

Most cheetahs live in parts of southern and eastern Africa. Many live in the African country of Namibia. Some live in the Serengeti National Park in Tanzania. This park is a **reserve** for wild animals.

Some cheetahs live in the Middle East, too. They live in an Asian country called Iran.

Cheetahs live on flat lands called **savannas**. Savannas have grass and some trees.

Many cheetahs live on the African savannas.

Hunting

Cheetahs eat meat. They often hunt Thomson's gazelles. They also eat antelope, impalas, rabbits, and birds.

Tigers and leopards often hunt at night. Cheetahs are different. They hunt during the day.

Gazelles are food for cheetahs.

Cheetahs quietly get close to their prey. This is called stalking. Stalking helps cheetahs catch prey by surprise.

Cheetahs and other cats often stalk their prey.

When cheetahs are close, they chase their prey. They trip the running animal. Then, cheetahs bite the prey's throat. This bite cuts off the prey's air. It will not be able to breathe. This is how cheetahs kill their prey.

Cheetahs drag their food to a hidden place. They must watch out for lions and hyenas. They will steal the cheetah's food.

Some cheetahs go hunting as a group.

A Cheetah's Life

Cheetahs are active during the day. They hunt at sunrise and sunset. Cheetahs commonly rest during the hot afternoon.

These cheetahs are resting.

Female adult cheetahs without cubs often live alone. Some male adult cheetahs live with other males. They form small groups called coalitions. A cheetah coalition may have two or four cheetahs. The coalition members are often brothers. They work together to hunt for prey.

Cheetahs do not roar. They call to each other with "chirping" sounds. Cheetahs can hiss, too.

Cubs

Female cheetahs can have as many as five cubs at one time. Newborn cubs are blind and helpless. They weigh about 12 ounces (340 g) each. Cubs drink their mother's milk. After five weeks, they can eat meat.

Lions, hyenas, and other animals kill cheetah cubs. So, the mother cheetah hides her cubs. She moves them to different hidden places.

Cheetah cubs

Cubs grow quickly. They watch their mother hunt. By the age of two, cheetahs can live on their own. In the wild, cheetahs may live for about seven years.

No More Cheetahs?

Cheetahs are in danger of dying out. There may be less than 15,000 cheetahs left in the world. Some people kill cheetahs for their fur. Some cheetahs die inside traps set by farmers.

Some people kill cheetahs for their spotted fur.

People are trying to help cheetahs. They are rescuing cheetahs caught in traps. They are teaching farmers other ways to keep cheetahs away.

This cheetah lives on a wildlife reserve.

Important Words

coalition a group of male cheetahs that live together.

cubs young cheetahs.

prey an animal that is food for another animal.

reserve a special park where animals can live in safety.

savanna flat land with grass and few trees.

stalk to secretly follow prey.

Web Sites

Index